"*Reconciliation Services for Children* fills a need at this time when the old Saturday confessional lines have dwindled, when emphasis has switched from a precise recitation of sins to a sense of reconciliation with a risen Lord, and people have discovered other ways of seeking and celebrating forgiveness.

"Gwen Costello has given pastors and catechists, teachers and parents a fine book of practical reconciliation services to teach children how to develop a proper conscience in relationship to the daily tensions and conflicts they encounter. She sensitively leads them to a correct sense of sin and the Christ who is always present with his gift of forgiveness. These services should prepare them well for faith-filled sacramental celebrations. I recommend this book and, as a pastor, am grateful for it."

William J. Bausch
Pastor and author, *The Hands-On Parish*

"In *Reconciliation Services for Children*, Gwen Costello offers 18 thoughtful, well-paced celebrations of reconciliation for use with children in grades two through six. In the process she shows herself sensitive both to the needs of 7-12 year olds and to the richness of the church's experience of reconciliation. Costello provides catechists, Catholic school teachers, and parish directors of religious education with welcome assistance in preparing children for their first experiences of sacramental reconciliation and in assuring them that the peace Jesus promised is always available."

Brian Haggerty
Co-author, *We Celebrate Reconciliation* and *We Celebrate the Eucharist*

"Gwen Costello's *Reconciliation Services for Children* may be used not only as part of a penance service in which reconciliation is celebrated, but also in the setting of classroom, home, or other gathering space as an experience of forgiveness for children even without sacramental absolution. The prayers and reflections are rightly focused for children in grade school. The optional activities are right on target for the age group.

"This book will be a valued aid to the catechist preparing children for penance and to the priest celebrating the sacrament with them."

Rev. William J. Koplik
Pastor and author, *We Celebrate Baptism* and *We Celebrate Confirmation*

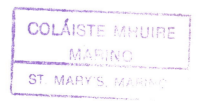

"DREs, catechists, school principals, and teachers are going to cheer when they see this new book from Gwen Costello. The services may be adapted to many settings; they may be used as part of the sacramental celebration of reconciliation in church, but they also will work well in church, classroom, or other settings where non-sacramental peace-making and reconciliation may be celebrated with children.

"Gwen Costello really knows children. This is evident in her use of words, stories, and delightfully meaningful activities to which children can relate and from which they can learn about and truly experience reconciliation. Anyone who prays with children, celebrates sacraments with them, or cares at all about their development as Christians will want to own and use this practical and inspirational book."

Peg Bowman
Author of *At Home with the Sacraments*

"A resource such as Costello's *Reconciliation Services for Children* provides the help needed by parish leaders in celebrating meaningful reconciliation rituals with children, in the church, classroom, and even in the home. The services are a well-designed blend of readings children will understand, responses in words that are natural to them, creative invitations to silent reflection, and optional activities that include various forms of creative expression. A valuable resource!"

Zeni Fox
Associate Professor of Pastoral Theology
School of Theology
Seton Hall University

Reconciliation Services for Children

18 Prayer Services to Celebrate God's Forgiveness

GWEN COSTELLO

TWENTY-THIRD PUBLICATIONS
Mystic, Connecticut 06355

Twenty-Third Publications
P.O. Box 180
185 Willow Street
Mystic, CT 06355
(203) 536-2611
800-321-0411

ISBN: 0-89622-516-x
Library of Congress Catalog Card Number: 92-60230

Contents

Introduction

I don't remember my "first confession," as we called it then, but I do remember something that happened shortly thereafter.

I was in third grade, lined up at the back of the church with my classmates waiting my turn in the confessional. I was nervous, afraid that I would forget my sins and the Act of Contrition.

When it was almost my turn, the priest startled me by poking his head out of the confessional. Something was definitely wrong. He beckoned to our teacher, Sister Mary Alacoque. She meekly moved over close to the priest and they conferred. Then he abruptly closed his curtain, and she, no longer meek, stormed over to those of us still in line. "Don't say the Morning Offering!" she hissed.

Oops! We had just learned this new prayer and apparently one after another of us had said it instead of the Act of Contrition. The priest was tired of correcting us. Now I was even more nervous. What if I said the wrong prayer? (I can't remember if I did or didn't.)

Clear-Cut Preparation

In spite of such occasional embarrassments, teachers and catechists in my day had it fairly easy when it came to preparing children for confession. At least it was clear cut. They taught us the unvarying formula: "Bless me, Father, for I have sinned...." They helped us memorize the Act of Contrition, and they guided us through an examination of conscience by reading us a list of sins before we went into church. Most confessors gave routine penances like "five Our Fathers and five Hail Marys," which we said immediately after confession. It was all pretty cut and dried. No surprises, no variation of the routine.

Today, of course, children are taught about penance, or reconciliation, differently and in a much less rigid way. They are taught from the beginning that they will be encountering a loving and forgiving God in this sacrament. The confessor's role takes a back seat to God's, and children don't worry as much about the priest's reaction to their sins. The emphasis is on sorrow and forgiveness, not on the correct recitation of facts, sins, and prayers.

While this is good news for children, it makes the role of catechists and teachers more difficult. What to teach about sin and forgiveness is not as clear. Which confession formula to use, if any, depends on the parish priest, as do the penances the children will perform. Will they learn a formal Act of Contrition, or will they express sorrow in their own words? Will they use a reconciliation room, a screen, or the confessional? These things now vary according to local custom. It's no longer possible to "just line them up" for confession.

Today, particularly for first penance, parishes often plan reconciliation services with appropriate songs and readings and prayers. Parents and other family members are invited and involved. Indeed, often the whole parish is invited and involved. All of this means less predictability and more work for catechists, teachers, and DREs.

This new emphasis is, of course, a good and positive development. The extra preparation is well rewarded when children understand that sin, sorrow, and forgiveness all come down to a personal encounter with Jesus who loves them and calls them forth on their faith journey. Nevertheless, the extra preparation does fall to catechists, teachers, and DREs, and that's where this book comes in.

Intended To Save You Time

This is a book of ready-to-use reconciliation services. It is intended to save catechists and teachers time, time better spent preparing children to receive the sacrament. It is geared to children in grades two through six who are either preparing for first penance or regularly receiving the sacrament in the parish or school.

These services are all related to the sacrament of reconciliation in some way. All can be used as part of a penance service in which the sacrament of reconciliation is celebrated. But most can also be used in classrooms, homes, or meeting spaces, with or without an ordained celebrant. All of them focus on the reason for the sacrament: to put children right with God, with others, and with all created things.

These services acknowledge the reality of sin and sinful actions, though they aren't meant to induce guilt and they don't dwell on the negative aspects of a child's relationship with God. They acknowledge a child's need for forgiveness, for sorrow, for change and reform, and for growth. And they do indeed acknowledge a child's need for friendship with God, manifested through the presence of Jesus.

Suggestions for a related activity and directions for these are included with each service (immediately before the closing prayers). These activities are optional and, if used, should certainly be adapted to the age level and needs of individual classes or groups.

Also incorporated into each service is a period for silent meditation in which children are invited to use their imaginations and to encounter Jesus. These meditations often serve as a private examination of conscience.

The appendices at the end of this book offer information about the sacrament of reconciliation, an examination of conscience for children, and acts of sorrow or contrition.

May you and those you teach celebrate God's forgiveness often and well. And may you enjoy the peace offered by the resurrected Jesus to his less-than-faithful followers. "Peace be with you," he said. At the sight of him the disciples rejoiced. And he said again, "Peace be with you."

Note: Permission is granted to reproduce these services for the children and adults who participate in them.

1   *Each of Us Is Unique*

Background Notes: This service highlights the need for reconciliation as children relate to one another in their daily lives. It suggests that building relationships involves effort and care, and that reconciliation is integral to friendship. Celebrating reconciliation as a sacrament should really be a reflection of what we are already doing daily as Christians: freely offering love and forgiveness to one another as Jesus did.

The role of leader should be taken by you or another adult. The children can serve as readers. Practice with the readers beforehand. For the optional activity have available brown grocery bags, pencils, scissors, and tape.

Times for Use
Year-round and as remote preparation for first reconciliation

Gathering Prayer

Leader: Let us pray that God will be with us as we now think about ways to grow in friendship. May God open our minds and hearts and bless us with gifts of love and care. We ask these things in the name of Jesus, present among us.

All: Amen.

Leader: Most of us live in families and most of us have friends. Even in the most loving families and among the best of friends, there are sometimes misunderstandings, quarrels, and even fights. This is normal and to be expected because each one of us is unique. Each of us thinks and feels and acts in a unique way and family members and friends often think and feel and act in opposite ways. But what should we do when our personality bumps against someone elses? Listen for a clue in this reading.

Reader One: *A reading adapted from the letter of James (4:1–12)*
Where do the conflicts and disputes among you come from? Don't most of them come from your desire to get your own way? You want things your way and when you can't have it that way, you fight for it. Or you want what someone else has, and when you can't get it, you quarrel and fight.

Reader Two: But this is not God's way. When you feel yourself giving in to this behavior, draw close to God and God will draw close to you. God will raise you up when you are willing to admit that you need help to overcome your selfishness.

Reader Three: Above all, don't talk about others in hurtful ways. Those who spread gossip about others and tear them down are disobeying the law of God. You certainly should not judge others. God alone is the lawgiver and judge, so who are you to presume to know what's in another person's heart?

The Word of the Lord.

All: Thanks be to God.

Leader: James ends his letter by asking his readers to practice patience with one another. He says that Jesus will show us how to love one another as we should. Let us now ask Jesus for help. Close your eyes and picture yourself surrounded by your family members. Point out to Jesus the one you most need to be patient with. In your own words, talk to Jesus about this person and ask him to give you the gift of patience.
(Allow two to three minutes for silent prayer.)

Leader: Let us pray...

Reader Four: Forgive us, Jesus, when we forget that our parents, brothers and sisters, and friends are just as unique as we are...

All: Teach us how to grow in love.

Reader Five: Forgive us, Jesus, when we let our selfishness get in the way of getting along with others...

All: Teach us how to grow in love.

Reader Six: Forgive us, Jesus, when we talk about others and tear them down to make ourselves look better...

All: Teach us how to grow in love.

Sacrament of Reconciliation
(If your group is not receiving the sacrament at this time, go on to the activity below.)

Optional Activity

Give all participants a brown grocery bag, and invite them to draw a large outline of themselves, with hands outstretched. Have them decorate the outline by drawing in features and clothing or by writing within it some of their gifts and talents. Names should be visible somewhere on the outline and also the words: "I am unique." Then cut the outlines out and tape them together hand to hand until all are attached. As you say the closing prayer, have each participant stand behind and hold his or her outline.

Closing Prayer

Leader: God, our loving parent, you have given each of us a unique personality. We have all been gifted by you in special ways. Teach us to love and value one another and to accept one another as the unique persons we are. We ask this in the name of Jesus who is here among us.

All: Amen.

2   *We Are All Connected*

Background Notes: This service introduces the concept of reconciliation. Unless children recognize that they are in relationship to one another and to God, they won't feel the need for reconciliation. By emphasizing their connectedness to God and others, you can help them see the importance of offering one another mutual love and respect. The role of leader should be taken by you or another adult. The children can serve as readers. Practice with the readers beforehand and have supplies (strips of colored construction paper and tape) ready for the optional activity.

Times for Use
Year-round and as remote preparation for first reconciliation

Gathering Prayer

Leader: Let us bow our heads and open our hearts to God who is here with us. Let us pray for God's guidance and let us believe in God's love and care for us. We ask these things in the name of Jesus.

All: Amen.

Leader: We are gathered together
in the presence of Jesus to think about our lives
and how they touch God and all others.
We are all connected:
God, Jesus, Earth, us, and the people next to us.
We are all a family.

(Stop here and invite the children to reach out and take the hands of the two people on either side of them. When everyone in the room has joined hands, say the following, inviting everyone to repeat after you:)

Leader: We are all connected.

All: We are all connected.

Leader: We are all a family.

All:	We are all a family.
Leader:	We are all children of God.
All:	We are all children of God.
Leader:	You may now be seated. Listen carefully to the following readings.
Reader One:	When we touch one another it's easy to see how our bodies are connected. It's harder to understand how we are connected "in spirit," but we are.
Reader Two:	It is true that what one of us does affects all of us. Even when we aren't touching others physically, our words are touching them, our attitudes are touching them, and our prayers are touching them.
Reader Three:	Paul talks about how we are connected spiritually in his letter to the Romans: Just as each of us has one body with many parts, and not all the parts have the same function, so, too, we though many are one body in Christ.
Reader Four:	We have gifts that differ, but we should all use our gifts to the best of our ability to build up the whole body of Christ. The Word of the Lord.
All:	Thanks be to God.
Leader:	Jesus is here with us. Close your eyes and picture yourself standing near him. He reaches out and takes your hand, and he invites you to take the hand of the person next to you. But you see that the person next to you is someone you have problems with. Talk to Jesus about this person now. *(Allow two to three minutes for silent prayer.)*
Leader:	Let us pray. Jesus, help us to use the gifts God has given us to reach out to others, even those we have problems with. Show us

how to form new connections with one another every day. We ask these things in the name of the Father, and of the Son, and of the Holy Spirit.

All: Amen.

Sacrament of Reconciliation
(If your group is not receiving the sacrament at this time, go on to the activity below.)

Optional Activity
Give each participant a 2" x 11" strip of colored construction paper. Ask each to put his or her name on the strip and to decorate it. Begin connecting these strips by taping your own strip end to end (your name on the outside) and inviting the person next to you to link his or her strip within yours and then tape it. When all the strips are connected, have two children hold the circle of strips as you pray the closing prayer.

Closing Prayer

Leader: Jesus, you are here with us.

All: Jesus, you are here with us.

Leader: We are all connected to you.

All: We are all connected to you.

Leader: We are all one family.

All: We are all one family.

Leader: Amen.

All: Amen.

3   *God Knows Us Very Well*

Background Notes: The more intimately we know people, the more we know their faults. This does not make relationships a negative experience. On the contrary, when people love us just as we are, they are able to accept our faults while at the same time challenging us to be the best we can.

It's important to help children view God as someone who knows and loves them intimately and unconditionally. God is not to be feared, but to be loved back. God reaches out and embraces us in our totality: strengths and weaknesses, good points and bad.

This service calls attention to God's presence and unconditional love. The readings and refrain are adapted for children from Psalm 139. Have paper and pencils available for the optional activity.

Times for Use
Year-round and as remote preparation for first reconciliation

Gathering Prayer

Leader: The Lord be with you.

All: And also with you.

Leader: Let us pray. Dear God, you tell us in Scripture that you are as close to us as our own heartbeat. You know us, just as we are, and you love us. Help us to believe that you are with us always, and teach us to respond to your love by being the best we can be. We ask this in the name of Jesus, your son.

All: Amen.

Reader One: Oh God, you know me so well,
you know when I sit and when I stand,
you know my thoughts before I think them.

All: Oh God, you know me and you love me.

Reader Two: You know when I go out,
and you know when I am at home.

	You know everything about me. Even before a word is on my tongue, you know what I will say.
All:	Oh God, you know me and you love me.
Reader Three:	You are in front of me and behind me and you rest your hand upon me. Knowing this is incredible. I can hardly believe that you care for me so much.
All:	Oh God, you know me and you love me.
Reader Four:	You have created me inside and out; even before I was born you knew me. I give thanks to you that I am so wonderfully made. All that you have created is wonderful.
All:	Oh God, you know me and you love me.
Reader Five:	Please keep close to me, God, and keep on knowing what is in my heart. Guide my thoughts and keep me on a straight path. Lead me toward you in all that I do.
All:	Oh God, you know me and you love me.

Leader:	I invite you now to close your eyes and picture yourself next to Jesus. He reaches out and takes your hand and you feel warm and safe with him. Share with him now whatever is in your heart:
	    Tell him about something that is particularly difficult for you right now....
	    Tell him about a failure you have had recently....
	    Ask him to help you to respond to God who knows you so well and loves you so dearly.
	(Allow time for silent prayer.)

Sacrament of Reconciliation
(If your group is not receiving the sacrament at this time, go on to the activity below.)

Optional Activity
Invite the children to write a contemporary song of praise, a con-

temporary psalm, that praises God for some gift in their lives. Suggest that they limit these psalms to five lines or so. Topics might be: a good friend, loving parents, a favorite food, a special activity, a hobby, etc. Show them a sample psalm, such as the following:

Oh God, I love to play.
Everyday I play with my friends.
We run, we jump, we chase one another.
Thank you, God for the gift of friends.

Closing Prayer

Leader: God, we have received so many good things from you. We have received the gift of life. We thank you for this and all your gifts, and we offer you glory as we pray…

All: Glory be to the Father,
and to the Son,
and to the Holy Spirit,
as it was in the beginning,
is now, and ever shall be,
worlds without end. Amen.

Note: If you have done the optional activity, invite children to share their contemporary psalms with one another now. Encourage them to take these home to also share with parents and siblings.

4   *Where Are You, Jesus?*

Background Notes: This service helps children reflect on the presence of Jesus here and now. It leads them to the conclusion that how they relate to those around them is how they relate to Jesus. It is ideal for helping them examine their behavior toward others. Explain before the service that sin upsets the balance of our relationship with God and Jesus. To make that relationship "right" (in other words, to be reconciled with God and Jesus), we must balance our relationships with the people around us.

Practice the verse recited by "All" beforehand and also practice with the readers. Have available paper, crayons or markers, and tape for the optional activity.

Times for Use
Year-round and as remote preparation for first reconciliation

Gathering Prayer

Leader: Jesus, you are here with us. You promised your followers that you would never leave them, and that promise extends to us, too. You are here with us through your Holy Spirit. We don't see your Spirit, but our faith tells us that your Spirit is real. Fill our hearts with love as we now pray and think together about our relationship with you, with God the Father, and with your Holy Spirit.

Reader One: After he died on the cross and was raised to new life, Jesus ascended to heaven. Before he left, he promised his followers that he would remain with them always. He would send them a helper and friend to keep his presence alive. But the followers wondered: How can we know that Jesus is with us if we can't see him? They gathered together in the Upper Room to pray about this.

All: Where are you, Jesus? We can't see you.

Reader Two: One day as they prayed, there was a noise from the sky that sounded like a strong wind blowing, and it filled the whole house. Then they saw what looked like tongues of fire spreading out, and each person there was touched by a tongue. They were all filled with the Holy Spirit.

All:	Where are you, Jesus? We can't see you.
Reader Three:	Some of the early followers tried to understand this great mystery. How does the Holy Spirit make Jesus present? Saint John explains it this way: No one has ever seen God, but if we love one another God lives in us. Whoever declares that Jesus is the Son of God, God lives in that person. It is the Spirit who puts this faith in our hearts.
All:	Where are you, Jesus? We can't see you.
Reader Four:	John goes on to say: This is the command that Jesus gives us, to love one another. When we do this, we are loving God. We can't say that Jesus is among us if we hate the people around us. When we love one another, our lives are in God and in Jesus. It is the Spirit who gives us the power to love.
All:	Where are you, Jesus? We can't see you.
Reader Five:	Paul, like John, puzzled over this mystery. He was a great follower of Jesus, but not at first. Paul, first known as Saul, was converted in a very strange way. One day he was on his way to the city of Damascus where he would be ordering the arrest of Christians. He was thrown off his horse and a voice called out to him: "Saul, Saul, why are you persecuting me?"
All:	Where are you, Jesus? We can't see you.
Reader Six:	Paul was astonished. "Who are you?" he cried out. The voice answered, "I am Jesus, the one you are persecuting." Paul thought about this for a long time. He eventually understood that Jesus *was* alive. He really *was* present in his followers. Paul never forgot this lesson, and he preached about Jesus from that time on.
All:	Where are you, Jesus? We can't see you.
Reader Seven:	Down through the ages, Christians have tried to understand how Jesus can be with us when we don't see him. We see signs of his presence and we feel it in our hearts, but we don't see him; we only see one another. People who have great faith understand that Jesus lives among us through others. How we treat others is how we treat Jesus.

All: Where are you, Jesus? We can't see you.

Leader: Let us now talk to Jesus in the quiet of our hearts. Close your eyes and picture Jesus knocking Paul off his horse. Ask him about this. Picture him meeting you in the hall at school. Ask Jesus about this, too. Is he really at school with you? Does he ever do anything special to get your attention? Ask him to give you a strong faith so you will know that he is with you.
(Allow two or three minutes for silent prayer.)

Sacrament of Reconciliation
(If your group is not receiving the sacrament at this time, go on to the activity below.)

Optional Activity
Invite children to discuss the words they repeated during this service: "Where are you, Jesus? We can't see you." Remind them of the conclusions reached by John and Paul. If Jesus is living in the children and in those around them, how should they treat others? If they were to draw a picture of themselves reaching out to Jesus, how would they picture Jesus? Have each now do such a drawing. When all are completed, tape them together to form a mural. Invite the children to stand around this mural for the closing prayer.

Closing Prayer

Leader: Look at the person next to you. Shake that person's hand. Bow your head slightly in the direction of that person. He or she is a follower of Jesus, and Jesus, through the power of the Holy Spirit, dwells in that person.

Let us pray. Jesus, give us the gift of faith that we might believe in your presence among us and thus love and serve one another in your name. We ask these things in the name of the Father, and of the Son, and of the Holy Spirit.

All: Amen.

5   *Love Is Stronger Than Sin*

Background Notes: This service deals with the everyday conflicts children experience in their relationships with others. Childhood is filled with such conflicts. Rivalry, name calling, taking sides, resentment, jealousy, even physical force are all experienced from time to time in childhood relationships. It is important therefore to remind children of their Christian call to deal with others fairly, to get along, and to build one another up—in spite of obstacles.

If your group has difficulty in these areas, you might want to use this service as soon as possible and plan time for discussing the points it covers, especially the reading from the letter of John. Have available paper, pencils, and a container for the optional activity.

Times for Use
Year-round and as remote preparation for first reconciliation

Gathering Prayer

Leader: God, our heavenly parent, you know each of us by name and you love us in a very special way. Teach us how to imitate your love in our relationships with others, with our brothers and sisters, our classmates, and the kids in our neighborhood and parish. Even when it's hard, help us to offer love to others. We ask this in the name of Jesus, your son and our brother.

All: Amen.

Leader: Sometimes you don't have to do anything but walk out the door and other kids bother you. They call you stupid, or make fun of your clothes, or laugh at you when you make a mistake. Your first reaction is to get even, and who could blame you for feeling this way? And yet, what God asks of you is to return kindness for unkind words and to return good for evil. When we show love for others, we are also showing our love for God. Here is what God's Word in the Bible says:

Reader One: *A reading adapted from the letter of John (1 John 4:20–21)*
When people say that they love God, yet hate others, they are liars. Those who have no love for those they *can* see, cannot possibly love God whom they cannot see. The commandment we have from God is this: those who love God must also love other people.

The Word of the Lord.

All:	Thanks be to God.
Reader Two:	But my case is different. I went down to the brook to play and this kid threw a stone at me. When I yelled at him to stop, he cursed at me. I was really angry because I didn't do a thing to that kid. I was minding my own business. I just wanted to go out and play. I hate that kid.
All:	The commandment we have from God is this: those who really love God also love other people.
Reader Three:	Sometimes you can't love someone. There was this girl who said she was my best friend, but when another girl came along who had more spending money and better clothes, my so-called friend started ignoring me. She acted like we had never been friends. Once when I went up to her, she turned her back on me and made a joke about me to her new friend. I hate her now. I don't know why I ever thought she was my friend.
All:	The commandment we have from God is this: those who really love God also love other people.
Reader Four:	Does God really expect us to love kids who are mean to us? My older sister tries to get me in trouble every chance she gets. She just gets a kick out of seeing me get yelled at. She acts like Miss Innocent when I tell my parents what she does. She tells them I'm imagining things and they believe her. I hate my sister.
All:	The commandment we have from God is this: those who really love God also love other people.
Reader Five:	Wait a minute! What should we do when someone deliberately hurts us? How can we love that person? It's not fair for God to expect us to love people no matter what they do. How can it be fair?
Leader:	In the Scripture passage we heard from Saint John, he goes on to say this: God hears us whenever we ask for something. If someone hurts us, we should ask God to help us deal with that person lovingly, and God will answer our prayer. We belong to God, just as Jesus did, and Jesus will help us deal with the difficult people in our lives. It's hard to understand, but God *will* help us to overcome evil

with good and to offer love when someone hurts us. When we pray for the person who has hurt us, little by little our anger will fade away. Even if the person doesn't respond to our love, we are nevertheless showing our love for God.

All: The commandment we have from God is this: those who really love God also love other people.

Leader: Think of someone in your life right now who is hurting you and making you unhappy. Picture this person clearly and then in your own words tell Jesus about him or her. Share exactly how you feel. *(Pause for one minute.)* Now ask Jesus to bless this person and to put love in his or her heart. *(Pause.)* Ask Jesus to also bless and heal you, so that your anger and hurt feelings will fade away. *(Pause.)*

Sacrament of Reconciliation
(If your group is not receiving the sacrament at this time, go on to the activity below.)

Optional Activity
Give each participant a slip of paper and a pencil. After time for reflection, ask each to put on the slip the name of someone who is hurting them right now and then fold the slip so it can't be read by anyone else. Collect the slips and place them in a container. Have one of the children hold the container high as you say the closing prayer.

Closing Prayer
Leader: God, our loving parent, help us to believe that you can change hearts. Help us to trust that you will help the people whose names are on these slips to be more loving. Help us, too, to learn to offer love to others whenever we can. We ask these things in the name of Jesus, your son.

All: Amen.

6   *Making Our Own Decisions*

Background Notes: It's very difficult when dealing with children to judge where they are in their moral development. At any rate, we should be slow to judge their ability to make moral judgments. Are they *capable* of knowing right from wrong? Are they *fully aware* of the rightness or wrongness of actions when they do them?

Because a child has reached a certain age does not guarantee any particular level of awareness of the seriousness of his or her actions. This service offers children an opportunity to reflect upon the seriousness of some actions as opposed to others. It also recalls one of the conditions of serious sin: full knowledge of the wrongness of our actions.

Times for use
Immediate preparation for first reconciliation, year-round

Gathering Prayer

Leader: Jesus, you are here with us. We love you and we thank you for the gift of your presence. Guide us now as we think about the rightness and wrongness of our actions. Teach us to know the difference so we can change our lives and better love and serve others.

Reader One: *A reading adapted from the letter to the Romans (9:1)*
If I truly belong to Christ, I will always speak the truth and I will not ever want to lie. When I am guided by the Holy Spirit, the Spirit of Jesus, I will know in my heart that I am speaking the truth and doing what is right.

The Word of the Lord.

All: Thanks be to God.

Reader Two: We are Christians and we have been baptized into Christ. But baptism does not make us unthinking robots. Though Jesus is with us always, we must make a personal choice to accept his presence.

Reader Three: We are Christians and the gift of the Spirit of Jesus, the Holy Spirit, has been given to us. Yet, we have the freedom to reject this gift. We can turn our backs on Jesus and not listen to his voice in our hearts. When we do this, however, we no longer make decisions with Jesus' help. When we do this, we tend to make selfish decisions, thinking only of ourselves.

Leader: I invite you now to listen to three situations and to think about them in silence. Ask yourself: What would I do in these situations?

Reader Four: Bethany's mother gave her money and asked her to go to the store for a loaf of bread. Bethany bought a cheap loaf and kept the change, knowing her mother wouldn't notice. Her mother probably wouldn't have cared anyway. Was Bethany wrong? Why or why not?

Leader: Pause now and talk to Jesus about Bethany. Tell him what you think of her behavior. What does Jesus say back to you?

Reader Five: Larry often goes to the arcade after school. He saves his lunch money so he can play games. Both his parents work so they don't know that he does this. He doesn't mind skipping lunch and he tells his parents that he gets home late from school because he's studying with a friend. Is Larry wrong? Why or why not?

Leader: Pause now and talk to Jesus about Larry. Tell him what you think of Larry's behavior. What does Jesus say in response?

Reader Six: Cassy thinks Mass is boring so she purposely lets her mind wander while she acts like she's paying attention. She makes up stories for her journal and when she gets home she writes them down. Her parents always praise her for behaving so well and she always accepts their praise. Is Cassy wrong? Why or why not?

Leader: Pause now to talk to Jesus about Cassy. Tell him what you think of her behavior. What is his response?

Sacrament of Reconciliation
(If your group is not receiving the sacrament at this time, go on to the activity below.)

Optional Activity
Invite children to talk about the three scenarios the readers have described. Though none of these situations describes "serious"

sin, each does suggest that the child involved knew what he or she was doing and knew that it was wrong. Use these questions to invite discussion:

• If Bethany's mother didn't care about the change, why would it be wrong? What is stealing? Was what Bethany did a form of lying? What makes you think that Bethany knew her action was wrong? Should she confess what she did when she receives the sacrament of reconciliation?

• Is it wrong to skip meals? Why? Is it wrong to use lunch money in any way you want? Was Larry's lie to his parents harmless? Who did it hurt? Can something be wrong even if no one gets hurt? Should Larry confess these things when he goes to the sacrament of reconciliation?

• What could be wrong with keeping your mind busy during Mass—especially if Mass seems boring? Cassy *was* behaving well, so why shouldn't she accept her parent's praise? What could be wrong with this? Should she talk to the priest about this in the sacrament of reconciliation?

After your discussion, invite children to role-play these situations. What would they say to Bethany? to Larry? to Cassy?

Closing Prayer

Leader: Jesus, you are always with us. Teach us to hear your voice when you speak to our hearts. When your Holy Spirit speaks to us, help us to listen so we will know right from wrong. Forgive us for the times we have done something wrong, *knowing it was wrong*. We ask these things in the name of the Father, and of the Son, and of the Holy Spirit.

All: Amen.

7   *What Have We Done?*

Background Notes: The focus of this service is what used to be called the "matter" for confession. In other words, what is it that children should be confessing? No one can tell another person which of their actions are sins, because none of us can read another's heart or conscience. There is no way that we can judge if another 1) knew the seriousness of an action, 2) gave sufficient thought to what he or she was about to do, and 3) fully decided to do it, knowing it was wrong. However, we can guide others by helping them to reflect upon the meaning of their actions and the meaning of sin. This service will help children examine their consciences before receiving the sacrament of reconciliation. Have available some paper, pencils, and a container for the optional activity.

Times for Use
Immediate preparation for first reconciliation, year-round

Gathering Prayer

Leader: Jesus, you are with us at all times. You know what is in our hearts and minds. You know, too, the sins we commit, and in spite of what you know, you always love and forgive us. Be with us now as we look at our lives and think about our sins.

Reader One: *A reading from the third letter of John (3 John 11)*
My dear friends, do not imitate what is bad, but imitate what is good. Whoever does good belongs to God; whoever does what is bad has not seen God.

The Word of the Lord.

All: Thanks be to God.

Reader Two: Let us pause now and recall our actions. Each of us must decide in his or her own heart which of our actions should be confessed to the celebrant when we receive the sacrament of reconciliation.

Reader Three: At home with our families, have we shown love and respect for our parents, sisters and brothers? Have we accepted our share of family chores? Have we accepted family rules? Have we respected the rights of other family members? Have we selfishly demanded things we didn't need from our parents, like expensive clothes, games, tapes, or jewelry?

Reader Four: At school with our teachers and classmates, have we been helpful and cooperative? Have we respected the rights of others? Have we done homework and class assignments properly and promptly? Have we obeyed school and class rules?

Reader One: In our parish and in church, have we listened and learned about God? Have we been quiet and respectful during Mass? Have we been cooperative during religion class and respectful of the rights of our catechist and the other children? Have we offered to serve the needs of the poor, the sick, and the elderly in any way?

Reader Two: In our neighborhood, town, or city, have we respected the property of others? Have we been friendly and helpful to our neighbors? Have we kept parks and public streets clean of our personal trash? Have we helped our families recycle trash?

Reader Three: For ourselves personally, have we tried to eat properly and get sufficient exercise? Have we tried to avoid unhealthy snacks and sweets? Have we shared allowance money with others? Have we spent money foolishly or selfishly? Have we wasted time watching TV when we should have been doing other things?

Reader Four: With our friends, have we been helpful and loyal? Have we given good example? Have we avoided bad language and bad habits? Have we put others down? Have we helped friends to feel good about themselves and their actions?

Reader Five: In our relationship with God, have we talked to God often: when we get up, before school, throughout the day, before and after meals, at bedtime? Have we remembered that God is always with us through Jesus and the Holy Spirit? Have we offered prayers of praise and thanksgiving for the good things in our lives?

Leader: Let us now spend quiet time talking to Jesus about these questions and about other areas of our lives in which we have failed to love God and others. Close your eyes and picture Jesus sitting next to you, listening.
(Allow two or three minutes for silent prayer.)

Sacrament of Reconciliation
(If your group is not receiving the sacrament at this time, go on to the activity below.)

Optional Activity
Give participants a piece of paper and ask them to write down one thing they have done lately that they are not proud of, something they feel is "matter" for the sacrament of reconciliation. They should fold the papers in half and not put names on them. Collect these in a special container and ask one of the children to hold it high as you pray the closing prayer.

Closing Prayer

Leader: God, you have told us through your son Jesus that our sins, no matter how great they are, will be forgiven because you love us more than we can imagine. Because we believe this, we will put aside our failings now and move forward with Jesus who lives and reigns with you forever and ever.

All: Amen.

Note: If you have done the optional activity, empty the container from your prayer table into a trash bag, explaining to the children that once their sins are forgiven they can "throw them away" and begin anew.

8   *Giving Good Example*

Background Notes: The purpose of this service is to alert children to their responsibility to give witness to their faith and to give good example to one another. Indirectly it focuses on sins of omission, things they *should be doing*, but aren't. It is not enough to refrain from giving bad example in our lives; we Christians must give good example by the way we imitate Jesus. We are called to be active in our faith, not passive.

For the Optional Activity you will need pieces of paper and pencils for each child.

Times for Use
Year-round and as remote preparation for first reconciliation

Gathering Prayer

Leader: The peace of Christ be with you.

All: And also with you.

Leader: May the love and unity that comes from our God, Father, Son, and Holy Spirit, be in our hearts and minds as we now reflect and pray together.

All: Amen. So be it. Amen.

Leader: We have received from God at baptism the call to be a family of faith who offer peace and reconciliation to one another. Though we are a family, each of us is special and unique. There is no other person exactly like us anywhere in the world. But all of us have the same call from God, which we must live out in our own individual ways. Saint Paul describes this call in a letter to Timothy.

Reader One: *A reading adapted from Paul's first letter to Timothy (6:11–12)*
You are the chosen ones of God and so you must turn away from the evil that you see all around you. Instead, try to be good and honest people who use God's gifts of piety, faith, love, and forgiveness as well as you can. Be people who deal with one another in gentle and understanding ways.

Leader:	In this letter to his friend and young disciple Timothy, Paul goes on to explain what it is we Christians must do in our daily lives.
Reader Two:	Continue to have faith in God, no matter how hard this may sometimes be. Keep believing that God has promised everlasting life and share this belief with those around you. I charge you to keep God's commands the best you can so that no one can criticize your behavior. Do all these things until our Lord Jesus Christ appears again among us. It is God who will make this happen. To God be honor and everlasting glory. Amen.

The Word of the Lord. |
All:	Thanks be to God.
Leader:	Let us now ask God for the help we need to get along well together in imitation of Jesus. Let us ask, too, for the strength to share our beliefs with others as Paul challenged Timothy to do.
Reader One:	That we might support and encourage one another to turn away from sin, let us pray to the Lord...
All:	Lord, hear our prayer.
Reader Two:	That we might use the gifts God has given us wisely and well, and never give bad example to others, let us pray to the Lord...
All:	Lord, hear our prayer.
Reader Three:	That we might treat one another with kindness and respect, and that God may forgive us when we fail to do this, let us pray to the Lord...
All:	Lord, hear our prayer.
Reader Four:	That we might continue—together—to follow Jesus in our world and share his message of love and forgiveness with others, let us pray to the Lord...
All:	Lord, hear our prayer.
Reader Five:	That we might encourage one another often to keep our faith in God alive and that God might forgive us when we are too weak to do this, let us pray to the Lord...

All:	Lord, hear our prayer.
Leader:	May God, who has called us to follow Jesus, strengthen our faith. Let us now, each in his or her own heart, ask God to forgive us for a time when we failed to give good example to someone close to us. Close your eyes and recall who that person is. Did your behavior cause that person to get in trouble? Picture Jesus watching you and this person. Ask him to forgive you for giving bad example, and ask him to strengthen you both to do better in the future. *(Allow two to three minutes for silent prayer.)*

Sacrament of Reconciliation
(If your group is not receiving the sacrament at this time, go on to the activity below.)

Optional Activity
Distribute the slips of paper and pencils. Ask children to think again of the person to whom they did not give good example. In his letter to Timothy, Paul wrote guidelines that Timothy could put into practice. If the children could write out one piece of advice for the person they have recalled, what would it be? *(No one should read these personal statements.)* Collect the slips and place them in a container. Have one of the children hold this as you pray the closing prayer.

Closing Prayer

Leader:	God, loving parent, Jesus, our brother, and Holy Spirit, our companion and friend, prepare our hearts to receive your forgiveness. Forgive us for the sinful things we do, but also forgive us for the things we *should* do and don't. Help us to follow Jesus always.
All:	Amen. So be it. Amen.

9   *God Always Forgives*

Background Notes: As children prepare for the sacrament of reconciliation, you should remind them often that they, too, can offer reconciliation to others. They can offer one another peace and forgiveness anytime, anywhere. This service reminds them of the importance of saying they are sorry for their sins, not just in confession, but in all the activities of their lives.

For the optional activity, have available a bowl of holy water and a small sprig of evergreen.

Times for Use
As immediate preparation for first reconciliation, Advent, Lent, year-round

Gathering Prayer

Leader: We gather together as God's children. Let us remember that God is full of gentleness and compassion for us. God knows us *as we are,* our good points and our weak ones. God strengthens us to do good, but also forgives us when we fail.

Reader One: For the times that we forget
that we are brothers and sisters
who should respect one another
and help one another,
Lord, have mercy.

All: Lord, have mercy.

Reader Two: For the times that we act selfishly,
putting our own concerns
before those of others,
Christ, have mercy.

All: Christ, have mercy.

Reader Three: For the times we have hurt one another
with our angry words or actions,
Lord, have mercy.

All: Lord, have mercy.

Leader: No matter what we have done, Jesus offers us the chance to try again. Saint Paul, one of his early followers, was responsible for the deaths of many Christians before he had a change of heart. Listen to what the Bible says about Paul, who was first known by the name Saul.

Reader Four: *A reading adapted from the Acts of the Apostles (8:1–3; 9:3–6)*
Saul approved of the murder of Stephen the deacon, and he tried to destroy the church. He went from house to house where Christians lived and dragged the believers out, both men and women, and threw them into jail.

Leader: Jesus forgave Paul's stubborn pride and his hardheartedness and gave him another chance. Listen now to how Jesus converted Paul.

Reader Five: On his way to Damascus, as Paul got near to the city, a light from the sky suddenly flashed all around him. He fell to the ground and heard a voice saying to him: "Saul, Saul! Why do you persecute me?" "Who are you, Lord?" he asked. "I am Jesus, whom you persecute," the voice said. Saul got up from the ground and opened his eyes, but he could not see a thing. He was blind.

The Word of the Lord.

All: Thanks be to God.

Leader: After several days, God told Ananias, a holy man in Damascus, to cure Paul's blindness and baptize him. Ananias said to Paul: "Jesus himself sent me, the one whom you saw on the road as you were coming here. He sent me so that you might see again and be filled with the Holy Spirit." After that Paul became one of the most faithful and energetic of Jesus' followers.

If Jesus could forgive Paul's sins, he certainly will forgive ours.

Let us now talk to Jesus about our need for his love and forgiveness because of the harm we have done to others. Close your eyes and picture Jesus sitting in your living room at home. Go sit beside him and talk to him about something that might be bothering you. Ask him to forgive you for any wrong you may have done this day.
(Allow two or three minutes for silent prayer.)

Sacrament of Reconciliation
(If your group is not receiving the sacrament at this time, go on to the activity below.)

Optional Activity
Invite children to stand in a circle. Ask one child to carry the bowl of water as you hold the sprig of evergreen. Move from child to child and lightly sprinkle each with the holy water. As you do so, say the following blessing: "_____, let this water remind you that Jesus forgives you just as he forgave Paul." When you have sprinkled each child, continue as below.

Closing Prayer

Leader: Let us now resolve to love and forgive one another, as Jesus forgave Paul. Let us offer one another this greeting: The peace of Christ be with you.

Response: And also with you.

10   *We Are Saints and Sinners*

Background Notes: It's very important to make clear to children that all of us are sinners. Jesus came to reconcile us with God, and by becoming one with us, he experienced the weaknesses we experience. He proclaimed that it was the sinners he had come to save. Those who are perfect have no need of Jesus.

We are indeed a church of sinners, in need of God's healing touch of forgiveness. Thus, it is not only okay to talk about sin with children, it is a disservice to them not to.

However, at the same time we acknowledge our need for God's healing, we should also acknowledge our call to be saints. Saints are sinners who steadily move toward God, in spite of their failings and weaknesses. Some of these people have been publicly acknowledged as saints, or canonized. The children in our classes are now in the process of becoming saints, of moving toward God through their daily lives. Our canonized saints can serve as models and inspiration for them.

For the optional activity, have available books or stories about one or several of the saints. Or, be prepared to share a story about a holy person living today.

Times for Use
On or near the feast of All Saints (November 1) and year-round

Gathering Prayer

Leader: Bless us, Lord Jesus, with your healing touch. You know what is in our hearts. You know that we are often weak and in need of forgiveness. But you came among us for just this reason, to lead us to God, to make us a holy people. Help us now as we reflect on ways to do this together.

Reader One: We rejoice in the people who surround us, Lord Jesus, but we ask your forgiveness for the times we have treated them poorly, Lord, have mercy.

All: Lord, have mercy.

Reader Two: We rejoice in your gifts of nature, Christ Jesus, but we ask your forgiveness for those times we have wasted or polluted these gifts, Christ, have mercy.

All: Christ, have mercy.

Reader Three: We rejoice in our possessions, Lord Jesus, but we ask your forgiveness for those times we have refused to share them, Lord, have mercy.

All: Lord, have mercy.

Leader: Jesus, we believe that you have forgiven our sins, but now teach us what we must do to be your holy people. Help us to keep moving toward you, in spite of the weaknesses and sins that slow us down. Be with us now as we recall two of your followers who were both saints and sinners.

Reader Four: When Francis of Assisi was a teenager, he thought nothing of spending money on expensive clothes and having a good time. He was very selfish and thought only of himself. He joined the army and went to war only because it seemed exciting, but he was wounded in the fighting and it took a year for his wounds to heal.

Reader Five: During that time he changed his ways. He met God very personally during his hours of recuperation. He became God's friend, and when his health improved he began to live a simple and even poor life, caring for the needs of others. He appreciated for the first time all the gifts of nature that God had created, and he felt at one with all created things.

Leader: Francis of Assisi, pray for us that we, too, will be God's friends who love and value all that God has made.

Reader Six: When Dorothy Day was a young woman, she led a wild life. While still unmarried, she became pregnant and had an abortion. Eventually she got married, but the marriage broke up after only one year. Then she fell in love with a man who was an atheist and they had a child. For reasons she could hardly understand herself, Dorothy decided to have her child baptized in the Catholic church. The man she loved was so angry about this that he immediately left her and the baby.

Reader Seven: After that, Dorothy's life changed drastically. She became a Catholic and began to devote her time and energy to helping the poor. She met a man named Peter Maurin who worked with her to begin a newspaper called *The Catholic Worker*. Together they opened over 30 Catholic Worker Houses of Hospitality for "homeless guests." Dorothy admitted openly that she was a sinner, but she believed in the forgiveness of Jesus. She did not let her sinful past stop her from becoming a holy woman.

Leader: Let us now talk to Jesus about Saint Francis and Dorothy Day. Tell him what you admire about them. Ask him to give you the help you need to turn your life over to him as they did. Talk to him about your hopes and fears and ask his forgiveness for your sins and failings.
(Allow two or three minutes for silent prayer.)

Sacrament of Reconciliation
(If your group is not receiving the sacrament at this time, go on to the activity below.)

Optional Activity
Invite the children to spend time looking at the books you have on display, or, tell them the saint story you have prepared. Ask if they have favorite saints or if they know any stories about saints they can share with one another.

Before closing, ask each child to think of a saint he or she can pray to during the closing prayer. This can be a patron saint or simply someone he or she admires.

Closing Prayer
Leader: Let us now take turns naming a saint. Each of us will say this person's name and the rest of us will respond: "Pray for us."
(When all have prayed, form a circle and join hands.)

Leader: Jesus, here with us, we join our prayers of praise to those of Francis of Assisi, Dorothy Day, and all the saints as we pray:

All: Glory be to the Father, and to the Son, and to the Holy Spirit, as it was in the beginning, is now, and ever shall be, world without end. Amen.

11   *Give Us Advent Hearts*

Background Notes: Advent is a time of anticipation and preparation for the birth of Jesus. It is a time for Christians to reflect upon what they can share with others in return for all the gifts God has given them, especially the gift of Jesus. Our culture offers a different message, however. It says: think about all the things you want, make lists, and make demands. There is no place for the babe born in Bethlehem in this scenario. There is only place for our greedy selves.

We have to make a special effort with our children during Advent to direct them away from selfish receiving to unselfish giving. Most of them *need* very little, but many in our world are in great need. This service directs children to reflect on the needs of others, and it suggests that they can best prepare for Jesus' birthday by reaching out to those in need.

For the optional activity, you will need old Christmas cards, glue, and scissors.

Times for Use
Before and during the four weeks of Advent

Gathering Prayer

Leader: Jesus, we have gathered together to prepare our hearts and minds to celebrate your birthday at Christmas. We want to think of things we can give you. Christmas is your birthday and we want to prepare presents for you. Help us to forget about ourselves for a while and to think only of you and how we can offer you love and joy.

Reader One: You'd better not pout, you'd better not shout; you'd better not cry, I'm telling you why...Santa Claus is coming to town.

Reader Two: Think about these words for a minute. They tell us to be on our best behavior, but why? So we'll get lots of presents, of course!

Reader Three: There are two things that make me sad about these words. One is that they tell us to be good just so we'll get presents, and the second is that they ignore the real meaning of Christmas. *We* get the presents, but it's Jesus' birthday. Does that make sense?

Reader Four: Well, it sort of makes sense. We exchange gifts with one another as a way of celebrating Jesus' birthday. But you're right! Come to think of it, all of us get presents, but Jesus gets none. If I had a birthday party and everyone got gifts but me, I'd be pretty upset.

Reader One: But what's the solution? How do we give gifts to Jesus? *(Invite responses from participants.)*

Leader: Some of you were right in saying that we can't give Jesus gifts directly. But remember what he says in the Bible: What you do to others, you do to me. That's why we give gifts to one another. It's a way of expressing our love for Jesus. The trouble is, we get carried away. We give and receive so many presents that we forget the love behind them. We forget why we're exchanging gifts, and we become very selfish.

Reader Two: What should we do? Should we tell our parents, relatives, and friends to forget about giving us gifts? *(Invite responses from participants.)*

Reader Three: Maybe the solution is to share what we have. We could share our gifts with people who need them. Then we would truly be giving a gift to Jesus.

Reader Four: This still sounds pretty hard to me. I like to keep my presents. I would find this really difficult, but I do see how important it is.

Leader: Sharing *is* difficult and it does take a lot of courage. It means that we will have to think about the needs of others and put our own wants aside. Let's pray about this now. Close your eyes and answer these questions silently.
(Pause briefly after each of these "examination of conscience" questions.)

• Is there a long list of things you want for Christmas?
• Is there something on your list that you could easily do without?
• Would you be willing to ask your parents to buy a gift for someone in need instead?
• Would you be willing to spend some of your own money to give a gift to someone in need?
• Do you ever think about Jesus as you prepare for Christmas?
• Do you talk to Jesus every day?
• Do you ask him to help you to think of others?
• What are you planning to do for Jesus on his birthday?

Picture Jesus now standing before you. Tell him how you feel about these questions. Which one of them in particular causes you problems? Ask for his help and guidance.

Sacrament of Reconciliation
(If your group is not receiving the sacrament at this time, go on now to the activity below.)

Optional Activity
Explain to the children that one small way they can begin to think of others this Advent is by making a card for someone who is lonely. They can write their own messages on these cards, offering the person their love and prayers. Explain that sometime before Christmas you will deliver their cards to people in your parish (or community) who will appreciate them.
(Allow sufficient time for making these cards.)

Closing Prayer

Leader: Jesus, teach us how to think about you this Advent. Teach us to reach out to others, to the poor, the lonely, the sick, and the hungry. When we give gifts to them, we are giving gifts to you. Help us to be generous. Help us to be strong.

We ask these things in the name of the Father, and of the Son, and of the Holy Spirit.

All: Amen.

12   *Jesus Is Among Us*

Background Notes: Christmas celebrates the Incarnation, the great mystery of God entering our world and dwelling among us. It is more than the birthday of the person named Jesus of Nazareth; indeed we don't know his historical birth date. Christmas is the birthday of God among us, when we are all offered new life in Jesus. Jesus the Christ is our Emmanuel, God with us. Thus this service focuses on the presence of Jesus among us, which we celebrate at Christmas. It invites children to think of Christmas as a time to rejoice in the presence of our savior who is always with us, loving us and calling us forth from our sins.

Have available paper, pencils, copies of the New Testament, and a large poster for the optional activity.

Times for Use
During the weeks of Christmas and year-round

Gathering Prayer

Leader: Jesus, we have gathered together to celebrate your presence among us. The real gift of Christmas is that God loved us enough to share you with us. Teach us to recognize this great gift and to grow in our understanding of it. Forgive us for the times we have ignored you and been ungrateful for the great gift of faith.

Reader One: *A reading from the Gospel of John (1:14-16)*
The Word became flesh and dwelt among us, and we have seen his glory: the glory of an only Son coming from the Father, filled with enduring love....Of his fullness we have all had a share—love heaped upon love....No one has ever seen God. The only Son, who is in the bosom of the Father, it is he who has revealed God to us.

The Gospel of the Lord.

All: Thanks be to God.

Reader Two: There once was a holy man named Meister Eckhart, who lived long ago in the 14th century. He thought a lot about John's words and the great mystery of God among us in Jesus. Here's what he wrote: "What difference does it make to me that Mary gave birth to Jesus all those years ago, if I do not give birth to Jesus every day of my life?" Meister Eckhart understood that Jesus is among us, his followers, and that we are the ones who show his presence day by day.

Reader One: John's Gospel says that Jesus reveals God to us, and Meister Eckhart says that we reveal Jesus to others. This is a great mystery. God has entrusted us with a great and noble task. But how can we do it? We are weak human beings who are selfish and sinful. How can we reveal Jesus to others?

Reader Two: Because we are human, we are sinners as well as saints. God knows us as we are and loves us just the same. It is the gift of God's forgiveness that enables us to proclaim Jesus. We are weak and selfish, but we can be forgiven. When we share with others the good news that our God is among us, loving and forgiving, we are revealing Jesus.

Leader: Let's think together about these things now in the silence of our hearts. Close your eyes and listen carefully. Think of something you did in the past for which you were particularly sorry. Was it something you did or said to your parents? Was it something you did or said to a friend? How did you feel afterward?

Did you ever talk to your parents or your friend about what you did? Even if you didn't, you can talk to Jesus about it now. Picture Jesus sitting in your living room at home waiting for you. His eyes light up when he sees you walk in. Talk to him about what you did in the past. Share with him any problems or weaknesses you are feeling right now. Ask him for forgiveness.

Sacrament of Reconciliation
(If your group is not receiving the sacrament at this time, go on now to the activity below.)

Optional Activity
Invite the participants to write in their own words a class code of Christian behavior. In other words, what do they think is required in order to reveal Jesus to others? Invite them to work in groups of three or four and suggest that each group think of two items for the code. Encourage them to use the New Testament, their textbooks, or any other resources you have available. Also remind them that their items should be realistic and do-able.

When the small groups have decided upon their items, write out the code on your poster. Refer to this code in future classes as a reminder of the call we share to reveal Jesus to others in our daily lives.

Closing Prayer

Leader: Jesus, we know that you dwell among us and that we celebrate this great mystery at Christmas. Because we are often distracted and selfish, however, we forget that you are with us and we forget that you have invited us to make your presence known. Teach us how to do this, Jesus. Help us to remember that you are with us always. We ask this in the name of the Father, and of the Son, and of the Holy Spirit.

All: Amen.

Note: If you have done the optional activity, also ask for the strength and guidance to live the items on the class code of Christian behavior. Recite each item and have the children respond: "Help us to live this daily."

13   *We Prepare for Lent*

Background Notes: Lent is a season of prayer, fasting (or penance), and self-giving (or almsgiving). It begins on Ash Wednesday and culminates in the joyful celebration of Christ's victory over sin and death at Easter. In the early church those who were to be initiated into full membership in the Christian community fasted during Lent as a preparation for the sacraments. At first the time of actual fasting was only two days, but by the fourth century an extended fast of forty days was usual.

Lent offers us and our children an opportunity to renew our baptismal promise to follow Jesus. We can look at our lives to determine if we are following Jesus faithfully or if we have developed habits that take us away from our Christian commitment. In the following service the focus is on renewing our baptismal promises in order to follow Jesus more closely. (The wording of the promises is adapted for children.)

For the optional activity, you will need pencils, index cards, a container, and holy water.

Times for Use
The week before Lent, Ash Wednesday, or during the first two weeks of Lent

Gathering Prayer

Leader: Jesus, you have called us to follow you from the moment of baptism until now. As we enter the season of Lent, help us to think about our Christian faith and to determine if we are living it as best we can. Please give us your help and send your Holy Spirit to guide us. We ask these things in the name of the Father, and of the Son, and of the Holy Spirit.

All: Amen.

Leader: When we were babies, our parents and godparents made promises in our name. Now that we are older, we can renew these promises ourselves. We can take responsibility for our call to follow Jesus.

Reader One: Our parents and godparents promised at baptism to turn our lives over to Jesus. Now we can do so on our own.

Leader:	Will you try this Lent to put yourself in Jesus' hands?
All:	We will try this Lent to put ourselves in Jesus' hands.
Reader Two:	When we were baptized, our parents and godparents asked forgiveness for their sins and they asked the church to pour the cleansing waters of baptism over us. Now we can ask forgiveness on our own.
Leader:	Are you sorry for your sins and failings?
All:	We are sorry for our sins and failings.
Reader Three:	When we were baptized, our parents and godparents promised to help us reject all that is sinful and to reject Satan who tempts us to stray from Jesus.
Leader:	Will you try to resist temptation and to follow Jesus closely?
All:	We will try to resist temptation and to follow Jesus closely.
Reader Four:	Our parents and godparents also promised to raise us in our Catholic faith, to believe in God, Father, Son, and Holy Spirit, and to place our faith in the teachings of the church. Now we can do this on our own.
Leader:	Do you believe in God, the Father, Son, and Holy Spirit, and in the teachings of the church?
All:	We believe in God and in the teachings of the church.
Leader:	We have now declared in our own voices that we will try to love and follow Jesus. Jesus is here with us now. Close your eyes and picture him sitting near you. Reach out and take his hand and tell him what is in your heart. Ask him questions about your baptism; ask him to explain anything you don't understand. Then be still and listen to his voice in your mind and heart. *(Allow two to three minutes for silent prayer.)* *Sacrament of Reconciliation* (If your group is not receiving the sacrament at this time, go on now to the activity below.)

Optional Activity

Give participants an index card and invite them to write a brief prayer to Jesus that expresses their desire to renew their baptismal call to follow him more closely. When all have written something, invite them forward one at a time with their cards. Place each card in a container and then bless each child with holy water while saying: "_____, remember your baptism and be thankful." Ask one of the children to hold the container high during the closing prayer.

Closing Prayer

Leader: Jesus, you have called us to come and follow you. In this container are our pledges to respond to your call and to love and imitate you. Help us to remember during the coming season of Lent that you are with us always. Help us to remember our promises. We ask these things in your name.

All: Amen.

14   *Keeping in Touch with God*

Background Notes: Three practices often recommended during Lent are prayer, fasting, and almsgiving. All three, of course, can be practiced throughout the year, but Lent is an excellent time to renew ourselves spiritually through these and other practices. Prayer in particular should receive our attention during Lent, since without it we are not communicating with God. Prayer has been defined many ways: as the lifting of the mind and heart to God; as an intimate conversation with God; as a heart-to-heart talk with God; and as silent listening. When we spend time in prayer we are keeping in touch with God and allowing God to keep in touch with us.

This service emphasizes the importance of prayer and encourages children to examine their prayer habits. It teaches them to rely on Jesus to lead them to God, during Lent and always.

For the optional activity, you will need a chart that says "Lent" in large letters.

Times for Use
During the six weeks of Lent and in Holy Week

Gathering Prayer

Leader: Jesus, you were sent from God to show us the way to God. Teach us now how to pray. Teach us how to communicate with God by placing ourselves next to you. You have promised that if we believe in you, you will dwell with us, and you have revealed to us that you and the Father are one. When you dwell with us, so does God. Lord, teach us to believe this, and teach us to pray. We ask this in the name of the Father, and of the Son, and of the Holy Spirit.

All: Amen.

Reader One: *A reading from the Gospel of John (14:1, 18-19)*
"Do not be worried and upset," Jesus told his followers, "just believe in God, and believe also in me. I will not leave you alone; I will come back to you. In a little while the world will see me no more, but you will see me; and because I live, you also will live. When that day comes, you will know that I am in my Father, and that you are in me, just as I am in you."

The Gospel of the Lord.

All:	Thanks be to God.
Reader Two:	I will not leave you alone, Jesus says; I will come back to you.
All:	Help us to believe, Jesus.
Reader Two:	Because I live, you also will live, Jesus says.
All:	Help us to believe, Jesus.
Reader Two:	Jesus says, You are with me, just as I am with you.
All:	Help us to believe, Jesus.
Leader:	Sometimes it's difficult for us to believe that God loves us so much. Imagine being given the gift of Jesus! But Jesus clearly tells us that he is indeed with us. The question is: How do we respond to him? Do we talk to him often and ask for his guidance? Or do we ignore him altogether?
	Close your eyes now and imagine yourself in a place you like to go by yourself. Picture Jesus there in that place waiting for you. Go and sit beside him. Tell him what's on your mind right now. Are you worried about anything? Tell him. Are you excited about something? Tell him. Are you sorry for something you have done? Tell him and ask for his forgiveness. Now just sit quietly and listen to whatever Jesus wants to say to you. *(Allow two to three minutes for silent prayer.)*

Sacrament of Reconciliation
(If your group is not receiving the sacrament at this time, go on now to the activity below.)

Optional Activity
Place the chart that says "Lent" in front of the children. Under this write Prayer, Fasting (or Sacrifice), and Almsgiving (or Service). Explain to the children that these three practices are important ways to observe Lent. Prayer keeps us in communication with God, fasting (or sacrifice) helps us to be strong enough to avoid temptation and sin, and almsgiving (or service) helps us to relate to all other people as sons and daughters of God.

Since prayer is really the virtue or practice that enables us to do the other two, invite children to brainstorm about where, when, and how they can pray during the coming week. As a group, choose one place, one time, and one way to pray and resolve to practice it at least once before your next class. Be sure to follow up on this throughout Lent.

Closing Prayer

Leader: Jesus, help us to remember that you are with us always. Strengthen our faith in God and in you. When your followers asked you to teach them to pray, you gave them these words. Be with us as we pray them now.

All: Our Father, who art in heaven, hallowed be thy name. Thy kingdom come, thy will be done on earth as it is in heaven. Give us this day our daily bread, and forgive us our trespasses as we forgive those who trespass against us. And lead us not into temptation, but deliver us from evil. Amen.

15 *We Share Easter Joy*

Background Notes: Because Easter is a feast observed in our culture only on Easter Sunday, though it is observed for six weeks in the church, it's particularly important to prepare for and celebrate it with our children. It is indeed the greatest feast of the church year since all of the events recorded in the Gospels lead up to and point toward the resurrection. Jesus suffered, died, and was buried, but he was raised up on the third day. This is part and parcel of our Christian faith.

Saint Paul pointed out to the Christians at Corinth (1 Corinthians 15:12–19) that without the resurrection there is no Christian faith. He declared that if Jesus were not raised up, our faith is for nothing. He said that since Jesus has been raised up, we who believe in him will be, too. This is an essential teaching of our faith.

Though all of us are day by day moving toward our own resurrection, sin is still part of our lives. Jesus came to save sinners, and we still have need of him on our faith journey. This service emphasizes our great call to follow Jesus and to share the joy of his resurrection. It encourages children to examine their lives and to reflect on daily ways to grow in faith.

Times for Use
From Easter to Pentecost and year-round

Gathering Prayer
(adapted from the *Te Deum*)

Leader: You, Christ, are the King of glory,
eternal son of the Father.
When you became man to set us free,
you did not turn away from Mary's womb.

Reader One: You overcame the sting of death
and opened the kingdom of heaven to all believers.
You are seated at God's right hand in glory.
We believe that you will come and be our judge.

Reader Two: Come, then, Jesus; sustain your people,
bought with the price of your own blood,
and bring us with your saints
to everlasting glory.

All: Glory be to the Father, and to the Son, and to the Holy Spirit. As it was in the beginning is now and ever shall be, world without end. Amen.

Leader: The Gospels tell us a great deal about Jesus, where he went and what he did and said. They tell us, too, that he was arrested, that he suffered and died on the cross, and that he was laid in a tomb. But they also tell us that Jesus was raised up by God. By his death and resurrection, he has set us free. The power of sin has lost its hold on us. Jesus has promised us new life. We, too, will share in his resurrection.

Imagine how surprised his followers were on that first Easter Sunday when they went to the tomb.

Reader Three: *A reading adapted from the Gospel of Mark (16:2–7)*
And very early on the first day of the week they went to the tomb when the sun had risen....And entering the tomb, they saw a young person sitting on the right side, dressed in a white robe; and they were amazed. "Do not be amazed," they were told; "you seek Jesus who was crucified. He has risen, he is not here; see the place where they laid him. But go, tell his disciples this good news. Jesus is risen."

The Gospel of the Lord.

All: Thanks be to God.

Leader: I invite you now to close your eyes and imagine that you are one of the people who have gone to the tomb on that early morning. What are you talking about as you go? What happens when you enter the tomb, expecting to find a body for anointing? What do you say to one another when you run out to find the disciples?

Tell Jesus now in your own words how you feel about the message from the angel: "He is not here; he is risen from the dead." Share with Jesus those times when your faith has not been strong, when you have failed to believe in his presence through your weakness and sin. Ask for his forgiveness now.
(Allow two to three minutes for silent prayer.)

Sacrament of Reconciliation
(If your group is not receiving the sacrament at this time, go on now to the activity below.)

Optional Activity
Invite the children to roleplay the resurrection scene described in the reading from the Gospel of Mark. Or, better yet, invite them to roleplay this scene in a contemporary setting. Tell them to

include what they would say to the disciples, once they found them. Afterward spend some time discussing these questions:

- What do you say to people today about the resurrection?
- Do you announce the good news in any way in your daily life?
- How might you begin to do this?

Closing Prayer

Leader: Jesus, though you have led the way for us, we often fail to follow. Although your messenger asked us to spread the good news of your resurrection, we often forget to tell it. Teach us how to love you and follow you as we should. Teach us how to give witness to you every day of our lives. We ask these things in the name of the Father, and of the Son, and of the Holy Spirit.

All: Amen.

16   *The Holy Spirit Walks with Us*

Background Notes: Pentecost is a special occasion to share with children the good news that God offers us unconditional love and forgiveness through the presence of the Holy Spirit. Jesus, not wanting to leave us orphans, sent the Spirit to remind us of all that he said, did, and taught. The Holy Spirit dwells in the church and in us, assuring us that God is always offering love, acceptance, and forgiveness.

Since the feast of Pentecost often falls in late May or June, celebrate this service sometime after Easter with your class, perhaps close to your last class of the year. Remind children that the Holy Spirit is with them always and that we celebrate this gift on the great feast of Pentecost. Have available blank, pre-cut pieces of cardboard (2" x 6"), and pencils or markers for the optional activity.

Times for Use
Before, during, and after Pentecost and year-round

Gathering Prayer

Leader: I invite you to say this prayer with me by repeating each line after me:

Come, Holy Spirit, creator blest,

All: Come, Holy Spirit, creator blest,

Leader: and in our hearts take up your rest.

All: and in our hearts take up your rest.

Leader: Come with your grace and heavenly aid,

All: Come with your grace and heavenly aid,

Leader: and fill the hearts that you have made.

All: and fill the hearts that you have made.

Leader: The church celebrates the feast of Pentecost fifty days after Easter. During the Easter season we focus on the resurrection of Jesus and his appearances to his followers after he was raised up. On Pentecost, we celebrate the presence of Jesus through the Holy Spirit. At the Last Supper, Jesus promised his followers that he would send them the Holy Spirit, *which is his own spirit,* as a way of staying with them.

Reader One: *A reading adapted from the Gospel of John (15:16-20)*
Jesus said to his followers: I will ask the Father and he will give you another helper to be with you always. This helper is the Spirit of Truth whom the world will not recognize, but you will recognize the Spirit, because it will be within you. See, I will not leave you orphaned; I will come back to you.

The Gospel of the Lord.

All: Thanks be to God.

Leader: After he had been raised from the dead, Jesus appeared to his followers and gave them the power to forgive sins, but he made it clear that they could only do this because of their faith in the Holy Spirit. Jesus was giving them the right to represent him and to offer his gift of forgiveness to people, but they could only do this if they lived in the presence of the Holy Spirit.

Reader Two: *A second reading adapted from the Gospel of John (21:19-23)*
Jesus came and stood before his followers and said: "Peace be with you." He showed them the wound marks on his hands and side, and they knew then that it was him. "Peace be with you," he said again. Then he breathed on them and said: "Receive the Holy Spirit. The sins you forgive in my name shall be forgiven."

The Gospel of the Lord.

All: Thanks be to God.

Leader: Let us now ask the Holy Spirit to guide us as we prepare for the sacrament of reconciliation. Please respond: Holy Spirit, come fill our hearts.

Reader Three: That we might believe in the promise of Jesus that he has given us the Holy Spirit to be with us always…

All: Holy Spirit, come fill our hearts.

Reader Four:	That we might be truly sorry for the times we have not lived in the presence of Jesus and his Spirit...
All:	Holy Spirit, come fill our hearts.
Reader Five:	That we might confess our sins with honesty and regret, and that we might turn back to God...
All:	Holy Spirit, come fill our hearts.
Leader:	Before we talk to the priest about our sins and our sorrow, let us first talk to Jesus. Close your eyes and picture yourself walking into the reconciliation room. Sitting there is not the priest, but Jesus himself! You go and sit beside him. He welcomes you and explains to you that later when you speak to the priest in confession, you will be also speaking to him. He has given the priest the permission to forgive you in his name. Tell Jesus now whatever is in your heart. Talk to him about what you will say to the priest in confession.

Sacrament of Reconciliation
(If your group is not receiving the sacrament at this time, go on now to the activity below.)

Optional Activity
Print the song/prayer with which you began this service on the board or on a poster. Invite the children to copy their favorite line or phrase onto one of the pieces of cardboard and then decorate and color it. They can use these as bookmarks, which will remind them that Jesus is present, always loving and forgiving them, through the Holy Spirit.

Closing Prayer

Leader:	Let us once again recite the words that opened this service: Come, Holy Spirit, creator blest,
All:	Come, Holy Spirit, creator blest,
Leader:	and in our hearts take up your rest.
All:	and in our hearts take up your rest.

Leader:	Come with your grace and heavenly aid,
All:	Come with your grace and heavenly aid,
Leader:	and fill the hearts that you have made.
All:	and fill the hearts that you have made.
Leader:	Filled with the Holy Spirit, let us now offer one another peace saying "The peace of Christ be with you."
Response:	And also with you.

17   *God Dwells in the Church*

Background Notes: This service is based on descriptions of the church from the *Constitution on the Church,* a document of Vatican Council II. Invite children to reflect on these images that show God as one who loves and cares for them unceasingly. As participants prepare for the sacrament of reconciliation, it is important to move away from the image that we are cowering sinners before an avenging terrible God. Jesus teaches through stories and parables that there are many ways to experience God as loving and forgiving through the church.

To prepare for this service, have available a table on which is placed a lighted candle, a copy of the *Constitution on the Church,* and a large sign or poster that reads: The church is God's dwelling place.

Times for Use
Year-round and immediately before or after the solemnity of Pentecost

Gathering Prayer

Leader: God, our loving parent, we are gathered here today to reflect on your presence in the church. You have called us through baptism and confirmation to follow Jesus, whose presence the church proclaims. Send us your Holy Spirit that we might better understand our own role in your church.

Reader One: The church is a sheepfold whose one and necessary door is Christ. She is a flock of which God promised to be the shepherd. Although guided by human shepherds, her sheep are nevertheless ceaselessly led and nourished by Christ himself.

Leader: Come, Holy Spirit; teach us to believe that we are led and nourished by Jesus.

All: Come, Holy Spirit, come.

Reader Two: The church is like a tract of land to be cultivated; it is the field of God. The church has been cultivated by the heavenly vinedresser and is now a choice vineyard. The true vine is Christ who gives life and fruitfulness to the branches, that is, to us.

Leader:	Come, Holy Spirit; teach us to believe that Jesus gives us life and fruitfulness.
All:	Come, Holy Spirit, come.
Reader Three:	The church has often been called God's dwelling place. It is also the place in which God's family dwells; it is the household of God where Jesus welcomes and embraces each person in God's name.
Leader:	Come, Holy Spirit; teach us to believe that Jesus welcomes and embraces us.
All:	Come, Holy Spirit, come.
Reader Four:	The church is also called our mother. She it was whom Christ loved.... He filled her with heavenly gifts for all eternity, in order that we might know the love of God and of Christ for us, a love that surpasses all knowledge.
Leader:	Come, Holy Spirit; teach us to believe that Jesus' love for us is beyond anything we can understand or imagine.
All:	Come, Holy Spirit, come.
Leader:	Let us now pray in the silence of our hearts, asking for the gifts we need from Jesus to believe that through his church we can receive love and forgiveness. Close your eyes and picture Jesus sitting in the front pew of your parish church. Go up and sit next to him. Tell him how you feel about being in church. Tell him about times you may not have paid attention and about times when your behavior may have distracted others. Ask him to help you to think about church in a different way, as a place where you can meet him. Ask for his forgiveness for the times you have not attended church properly. *(Allow two or three minutes for silent prayer.)*

Optional Activity

Lead participants through a brief examination of conscience based on the descriptions of the church just read. For example, you might say:

• Do I believe that Jesus is with me? Do I believe that just as shepherds watch over their sheep, Jesus watches over me?

• Are there ways I cut myself off from the church? Are there ways I refuse the gifts of life that Jesus, the true vine, offers me?

• When I am in church, do I consider it a dwelling place of God? Do I treat other people as if God dwells in them?

• Are there gifts Jesus has given me that I don't use? Are there gifts I have wasted or used to hurt others?

• Do I believe that God, Father, Son, and Spirit, loves me unconditionally? Do I respond to this love daily?

Sacrament of Reconciliation
If your group is not receiving the sacrament at this time, go on to the closing prayer.)

Closing Prayer

Leader: Jesus, here among us, your presence tells us that we, too, are the church. We are the dwelling place of God. It is in us and through us that you express your love for us and others. Teach us to love and forgive one another in imitation of you. We ask you this in the name of the Father, and of the Son, and of the Holy Spirit.

All: Amen.

18 *God's Forgiveness Is Free*

Background Notes: Salvation and repentance are difficult concepts for children as well as adults. We get bogged down by our sins and consider the task of repentance too difficult if it means that we must change our lives before we can "win" the gift of salvation. But this thinking is backwards. We already have the gift of salvation; Jesus has earned it for us and God gives it to us unconditionally. Repentance is our response to God's free gift. We repent, or in other words "turn our lives around," because we want to *respond* to God's love, not because we are trying to win God's love. Our task is simply to respond to what is already offered. This service assures children that Jesus is always with them to teach them how to respond to God's unconditional love and forgiveness. Have available paper, pencils, and a container for the optional activity.

Times for Use
Year-round, Advent, Lent, and during immediate preparation for first reconciliation

Gathering Prayer

Leader: Jesus, we believe that you are here with us and we thank you for the gift of your presence. Bless us now as we pray and think together about your gift of forgiveness. You give it to us freely. Show us how to respond to it. We ask this in the name of the Father, and of the Son, and of the Holy Spirit.

All: Amen.

Leader: Birthday parties are lots of fun, and often relatives and friends give us special gifts. They give us gifts just because we are us, and just because we were born on this special day.

A few days after our birthday, it's the polite thing to do to send thank-you notes to those who have given us gifts. Kids often forget to do this. Has your mother or father ever had to remind you? Why do you think they want you to send these notes? *(Allow time for responses.)*

Reader One: Wouldn't it be a silly thing to send thank you notes *before* your birthday, before anyone has even given you anything?

People would think you were crazy, or maybe they would

think you were hinting that you want a present. Anyway, no one sends thank-you notes before a gift is given.

Reader Two: In a way, though, this is what we do to God. God gives us the gift of forgiveness, but before we receive it we think we have to send God a message. We think we have to be able to tell God that we will never sin again, that we are now as perfect as possible.

Reader Three: What must God think of this? God is saying, "Here, receive my gift," and we are saying, "Oh no, I can't take it until I do certain things to change my ways."

Reader Four: We have it backwards. We must first reach out and receive God's forgiveness and then respond to this great gift by turning our lives around toward God. The more God forgives us, the more we will want to get closer to God. What a great thing this is!

Reader Five: The sacrament of reconciliation is celebrated in the church to give people the opportunity to receive the gift of forgiveness that God so freely offers. It reminds us that God loves and cares for us and gives us forgiveness, whether we "deserve" it or not. The sacrament also teaches us how to turn ourselves around to God.

Reader Six: When we go to this sacrament we speak to the priest or celebrant who stands in for Jesus. This person speaks the words of forgiveness in Jesus' name and offers us suggestions about how we can respond even more to God's presence in our lives. Another name for these suggestions is "penance." After we confess our sins, the priest gives us a penance to say or perform.

Leader: When we think of this sacrament as a meeting with Jesus, and when we think of our penance as a chance to respond to God more fully, it becomes something we can look forward to. It's something like a birthday party where we receive gifts just because we are who we are.

As you prepare now for the sacrament, close your eyes and picture Jesus. He is surrounded by people who have come to listen to him. All at once a child runs up and tries to climb on Jesus' lap. The adults are annoyed and try to get the child away. But Jesus says, "Let the children come to me." He explains to the adults that children know how much God loves them and they don't worry about anything except receiving God's love. That's how everyone should be, Jesus tells the people.

Talk to Jesus about this now in your heart. Ask him to help you to learn to receive God's forgiveness and to respond by turning your life around to God. Ask Jesus to show you how you might do this.

Sacrament of Reconciliation
(If your group is not receiving the sacrament at this time, go on to the activity below.)

Optional Activity
Invite each child to write a thank-you note to God for the gift of forgiveness that God offers so freely in the sacrament of reconciliation and in countless other ways. Allow sufficient time for writing these notes.

Closing Prayer

Leader: We have talked to Jesus and we have learned that God offers us forgiveness, even before we ask for it. God freely forgives us in the sacrament of reconciliation, at Mass, and in many other ways in our daily lives. I invite you now to come forward with your thank-you notes.

As each comes forward, ask: "_____, do you accept God's gift of forgiveness?" (*Suggest that participants respond "yes" if they want, but don't coerce them.*) Then have each place his or her thank-you note in a container.

When all the notes are in the container, lift it high and say: Let us now praise God for the gift of forgiveness and for all that we have received:

All: Glory be to the Father, and to the Son, and to the Holy Spirit, as it was in the beginning, is now, and ever shall be, world without end. Amen.

The Rite of Reconciliation

Note: You might want to duplicate this information for each child and have them study it at home. Permission granted to duplicate.

Dear Child,

As you prepare to receive the sacrament of reconciliation (or penance, or confession, as your parents may call it), you should first spend some time thinking about what you will tell the priest. It's not necessary to tell every sin or fault, but you should mention faults and sins that you have the most trouble with. After you have thought about your sins and are sincerely sorry for them, you are ready to go into the reconciliation room, or confessional. Remember that there are six steps you will be going through as you receive the sacrament of reconciliation.

•The first step is called **Reception of the Penitent** (that's you). This simply means that when you enter the reconciliation room, the priest will greet you, to help you feel at ease. He may say "hello" or "peace be with you." Then he will invite you to make the Sign of the Cross, and he will ask you to believe in God's forgiveness.

•Step two is a **Reading from Scripture.** The priest might choose any text, for example, Isaiah 53:4–6 or Matthew 6:14–15 (if you don't know what these are, look them up). The priest might discuss the reading with you briefly. Don't be frightened by this; it's not a quiz, but rather an opportunity to share God's Word together.

•The reading is followed by the **Confession of Sins and Acceptance of Satisfaction.** Though this sounds complicated, all it means is that you tell the priest your sins and he listens in the name of Jesus. He may ask you to do something to show that you are willing to change your behavior. If you have learned a "formula" for confessing your sins, you may use it now, for example: "Bless me, father, for I have sinned...." Or you may tell the priest your sins in your own words.

The important thing is that you want to be a better Christian, and that you want to follow Jesus more closely in your daily life. After listening to you, the priest will suggest that you do some action or say some prayer as a response to what you have done. This is called your penance.

•The fourth step is the **Expression of Sorrow.** You tell the priest that you are truly sorry for your sins, either by reciting a formal prayer, such as the Act of Contrition, or by saying a prayer of sorrow in your own words. The priest will not be concerned about how well you recite the Act of Contrition. Rather, his concern will be that you are truly sorry for your sins.

•Step five is called **Absolution.** The priest will extend his hands over you as he prays in these words that you will receive God's forgiveness: "I absolve you from your sins in the name of the Father, and of the Son, and of the Holy Spirit...."

•The final step is called the **Proclamation of Praise of God and Dismissal.** It does seem fitting that you should praise God after having received forgiveness, doesn't it? The priest will help you out by saying something like this: "Go in peace, and proclaim to the world the wonderful works of God, who has brought you salvation." You can answer "Amen." Then you simply say thank you and leave the reconciliation room.

As soon as possible you should do the action or say the prayers the priest has given you. And, if possible, after receiving the sacrament of reconciliation, you should spend a little time talking to God in your own words.

An Examination of Conscience

(for children in grades two through five)

When we prepare to receive the sacrament of reconciliation, it's important to think about what we want to say to the celebrant. And yet, we don't need to carry with us a long list of sins and failings. All of us could do that because all of us are sinners. We all fail from time to time.

But that's not what we are asked to do in this sacrament. Rather, we are asked to think about those things that crop up over and over in our lives, things we can't seem to do right or to stop doing. It is these sins and failings that we should confess and it is for these in particular that we need God's love and forgiveness.

Listen now and consider some of the things for which you particularly need God's forgiveness.

• *How am I as a child of God?* Do I talk to God every day? Do I try to learn about God from my parents and teachers and from going to Mass? Do I remember that I am a child of God?

• *How do I act in my family?* Do I always try to get my own way? Do I help with family chores? Do I try to give joy to my parents and sisters and brothers? Am I grateful for all they do for me?

• *What kind of friend am I?* Do I play fairly and allow other children to share my toys and games? Do I keep secrets and do I defend my friends when others talk about them? Do I allow new kids to join my games or do I tell them to get away?

• *What kind of student am I?* Do I try my best? Do I cooperate with the teacher and with my classmates? Do I do my homework and other schoolwork the best I can? Do I ever cheat or disrupt the class?

• *Do I have serious faults?* Do I ever purposely lie or steal? Do I make up stories about others to get them in trouble? Do I demand expensive things from my parents? Do I destroy my own belongings or those of others?

• *Is there something I do often* that wasn't mentioned at all? What is it?

If you realize that you have failed in some of these ways, think of the one thing that keeps coming up over and over, and resolve to discuss this with the celebrant. Remember, however, no matter how many times you fail, God always accepts your heartfelt sorrow and forgives you. The important thing is to be aware of your failings and try hard to change. With God's help you can do it!

An Examination of Conscience

(for children in grades four through six)

When we prepare to receive the sacrament of reconciliation, it's important to think about what we want to say to the celebrant. And yet, we don't need to carry with us a long list of sins and failings. All of us could do that because all of us are sinners. We all fail from time to time.

But that's not what we are asked to do in this sacrament. Rather, we are asked to think about those things that crop up over and over in our lives, things we can't seem to do right or to stop doing. It is these sins and failings that we should confess and it is for these that we need God's love and forgiveness.

Listen now as we consider some of the things for which we need God's forgiveness.

•*At home with our families,* have we shown love and respect for our parents, sisters and brothers? Have we accepted our share of family chores? Have we accepted family rules? Have we respected the rights of other family members? Have we selfishly demanded things we didn't need from our parents, like expensive clothes, games, tapes, or jewelry?

•*At school with our teachers and classmates,* have we been helpful and cooperative? Have we respected the rights of others? Have we done homework and class assignments properly and promptly? Have we obeyed school and class rules?

•*In our parish and in church,* have we listened and learned about God? Have we been quiet and respectful during Mass? Have we been cooperative during religion class and respectful of the rights of our catechist and the other children? Have we offered to serve the needs of the poor, the sick, and the elderly in any way?

•*In our neighborhood, town, or city,* have we respected the property of others? Have we been friendly and helpful to our neighbors? Have we kept parks and public streets clean of our personal trash? Have we helped our families recycle trash?

•*For ourselves personally,* have we tried to eat properly and get sufficient exercise? Have we tried to avoid unhealthy snacks and sweets? Have we shared allowance money with others? Have we spent money foolishly or selfishly? Have we wasted time watching TV when we should have been doing other things?

• *With our friends,* have we been helpful and loyal? Have we given good example? Have we avoided bad language and bad habits? Have we put others down? Have we helped friends to feel good about themselves and their actions?

• *In our relationship with God,* have we talked to God often: when we get up, before school, throughout the day, before and after meals, at bedtime? Have we remembered that God is always with us through Jesus and the Holy Spirit? Have we offered prayers of praise and thanksgiving for the good things in our lives?

If you realize that you have failed in some of these ways, think of the one thing that keeps coming up over and over, and resolve to discuss this with the celebrant. Remember, however, no matter how many times you fail, God always accepts your heartfelt sorrow and forgives you. The important thing is to be aware of your failings and try hard to change. With God's help you can do it!

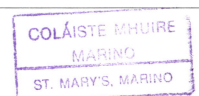

An Examination of Conscience
(based on images of the church)

When we prepare to receive the sacrament of reconciliation, it's important to think about what we want to say to the celebrant. And yet, we don't need to carry with us a long list of sins and failings. All of us could do that because all of us are sinners. We all fail from time to time.

But that's not what we are asked to do in this sacrament. Rather, we are asked to think about those things that crop up over and over in our lives, things we can't seem to do right or to stop doing. It is these sins and failings that we should confess and it is for these that we need God's love and forgiveness.

Listen now as we consider some of the things for which we need God's forgiveness.

The church is a sheepfold whose one and necessary door is Christ, the good shepherd.
•Do I believe that Jesus is with me? Do I believe that just as a shepherd watches over the sheep, Jesus watches over me?

The church is a choice vineyard cultivated by God. The true vine is Christ who gives life to us, the branches.
•Are there ways I cut myself off from Jesus? Are there ways I refuse the gifts of life that Jesus, the true vine, offers me through the church?

The church has been called God's dwelling place. It is God's household.
•When I am in my parish church, do I consider it a dwelling place of God? Do I show respect and reverence for the signs of God's presence there, for example, the tabernacle, the altar, and the Bible? Do I treat the people in church with respect as members of God's household?

The church is also called our mother. Christ has filled her with heavenly gifts for us to use.
•Are there gifts Jesus has given me through the church that I don't use? Are there gifts I have wasted or used to hurt others? Do I think of the church as a mother who loves and forgives me?

If you realize that you have failed in some of these ways, think of the one thing that keeps coming up over and over, and resolve to discuss this with the celebrant. Remember, however, no matter how many times you fail, God always accepts your heartfelt sorrow and forgives you. The important thing is to be aware of your failings and try hard to change. With God's help you can do it!

Acts of Contrition

•O my God, I am heartily sorry for having offended you, and I detest all my sins because of your just punishments. I firmly resolve with the help of your grace to sin no more and to avoid the near occasions of sin. Amen.

•Dear God, I am your child and I love you very much. Sometimes I am not the best child I can be, and I am sorry for those times. Forgive me, please, and help me to try again to love and serve you and others. Amen.

•I confess to almighty God, and to you, my brothers and sisters, that I have sinned through my own fault, in my thoughts and in my words, in what I have done and in what I have failed to do; and I ask blessed Mary, ever virgin, all the angels and saints, and you, my brothers and sisters, to pray for me to the Lord, Our God.

•Lord Jesus, we have sinned against you,
Lord, have mercy.
Christ Jesus, you came to call sinners,
Christ, have mercy.
Lord Jesus, you plead for us at the right hand of the Father,
Lord, have mercy.

•May almighty God have mercy on me,
forgive me my sins,
and bring me to everlasting life. Amen.

•Jesus, you told Peter that he must forgive others seventy times seven times; in other words, you told him to forgive others countless times. I ask you now, Jesus, to forgive me once again for my sins and weaknesses. You have forgiven me over and over, and I ask you again to give me your blessing of forgiveness and peace. Strengthen me that I might forgive others, just as you forgive me. Amen.

•Lord Jesus Christ, Son of the living God, have mercy on me, a sinner.

Other Books by Gwen Costello

Praying With Children

Twenty-eight prayer services for a variety of occasions. Covers the seasons of the year, liturgical feasts and special occasions. For teachers, catechists and parents.
ISBN: 089622-439-2, 96 pages, 8.5" X 11", Paper, $9.95 (order C-32)

Prayer Services for Religious Educators

Thirty-two prayer services for children, teens, parish ministers and families. Focuses on the liturgical year and the sacraments.
ISBN: 089622-390-6, 80 pages, 8.5" X 11", Paper, $9.95 (order W-93)

Stations of the Cross Booklets

A Bible Way of the Cross for Children
ISBN: 089622-353-1, 32 pages, 5.5" X 8.5", Paper, $1.95 (order W-26)

Stations of the Cross for Teenagers
ISBN: 089622-386-8, 32 pages, 5.5" X 8.5", Paper, $1.95 (order W-85)

A Way of the Cross for Religion Teachers
ISBN: 089622-429-5, 32 pages, 5.5" X 8.5", Paper, $1.95 (order W-31)

Videos by Gwen Costello

Maria's First Communion
VHS videocassette, $29.95 (order D.26)

Following Jesus Through the Church Year
8-part lectionary-based series, $29.95 each VHS videocassette
(order D-61 through D-68)

Lenny Learns About Lent
VHS Videocassette, $29.95 (order D-31)

Ricky's Reconciliation
VHS videocassette, $29.95 (call 1-800-321-0411 for ordering information)

Available at religious bookstores or from

TWENTY-THIRD PUBLICATIONS
P.O. Box 180
Mystic, CT 06355
1-800-321-0411